A Wind Chime

By Heather Hammonds

Photographs by Lyz Turner-Clark

Wind chimes make sounds on windy days.

This wind chime
is made with a long stick
and some string.

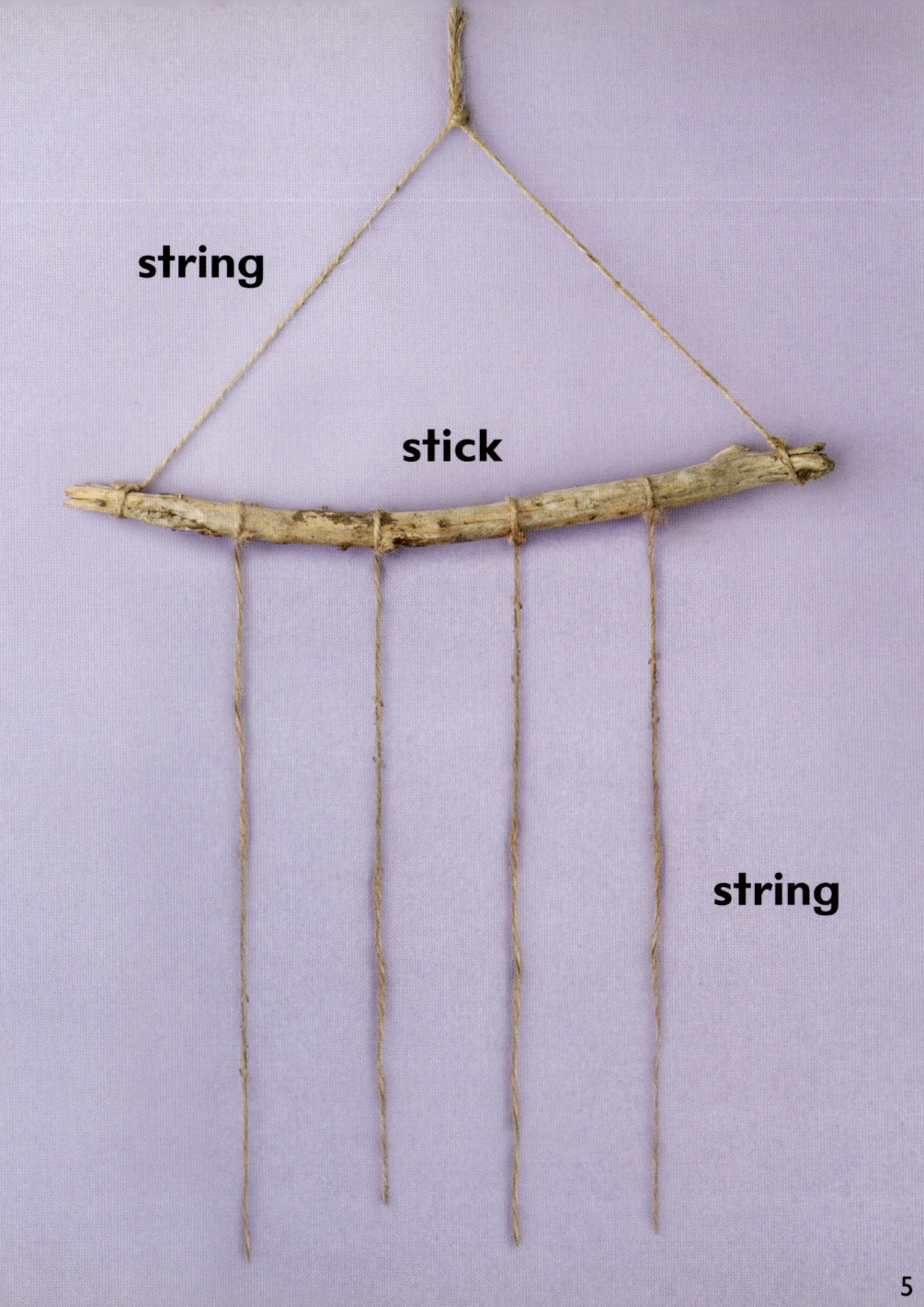

string

stick

string

Beads and feathers
are on the string.

Bells and a stone
are on the string, too.

bells

stone

beads

feathers

7

The beads on the string make a pattern.

Some of the beads glow in the dark.

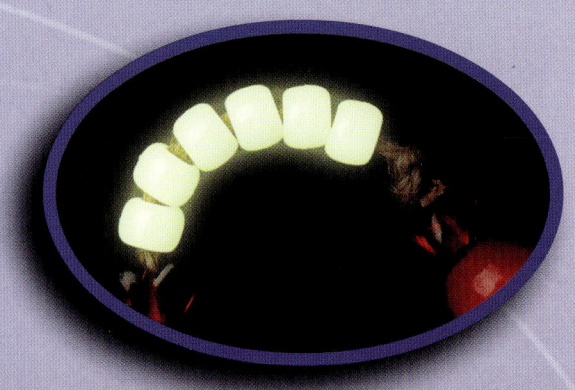

The wind chime
has lots of feathers.
The feathers are red,
white and blue.

Some feathers are long.

The wind chime
has eight bells.

Four bells are big
and four bells are little.

The wind chime
has four stones.

The stones are heavy.

The wind chime
is in a garden.
It makes a good sound
on windy days.